Celebrating Families

Rosmarie Hausherr

SCHOLASTIC PRESS / NEW YORK

I am most thankful to the children and the parents of the fourteen families who agreed to be photographed and interviewed for this book. They generously offered their time for the photo sessions and opened their homes to me.

A big thank you to my many friends in New York and in Vermont, who helped me find these families through networking. I appreciate the assistance I received from The Third Street Music School Settlement, NY; Sister Marie, McMahon Services for Children, NY; Sister Georgette, The Partnership for the Homeless, NY; Mikki Lam, Just One Break, NY; Julie Kempton, Stitches by Julianna, VT; Tula Hawkins Lacy, Administration for Children's Services, NY; Pine Street Co-housing, Amherst, MA; The Metropolitan Museum of Art, NY; North East State Correctional Facility, VT.

I am grateful to my editor Dianne Hess who has offered her strong support and good advice throughout this project. Many thanks to Marijka Kostiw, associate art director, and to the art department for a beautiful execution of the book.

Black-and-white family photograph on page 6 courtesy of Myles Pinkney.

LIBRARY OF CONGRESS CATALOGING-IN-PUBLICATION DATA
Hausherr, Rosmarie.
Celebrating families / Rosmarie Hausherr. p. cm.
Summary: Presents brief descriptions of many different kinds of families, both traditional and nontraditional.
ISBN 0-590-48937-2
1. Family—United States—Juvenile literature. 2. Problem families—United States—Juvenile literature. [1. Family. 2. Family problems. 3. Family life.] I. Title.
HQ536.H356 1997
306.85'0973—dc20   96-5036 CIP AC

12 11 10 9 8 7 6 5 4 3 2 1   7 8 9/9 0 1 2/0
Printed in the U.S.A.

First printing, April 1997

Book design by Marijka Kostiw

The text type was set in Veljovic Medium.

This book
is dedicated to
my wonderful family:
Vati; Mutti;
my sister Brigitte;
and my brother Beat.

Rosmarie

left: Leon; *right:* sister Charnelle; Daddy; Mommy; brother Rashad

Meet *Leon* and his family

RUTLAND FREE LIBRARY

Leon lives in a house in the suburbs with his parents and his younger sister and brother.

He does well in school and has fun playing soccer. He takes photographs and plays chess with his father, who is a photographer. Leon draws and paints like Grandpa, Uncle Scott, and Uncle Brian, who are all artists. The family reads the Bible together, and Leon sings in the choir. Family holidays are celebrated at his grandparents' house with all of his aunts, uncles, and cousins.

left: Joseph; *standing:* Grandma; Grandpa; brother Nicholas; Aunt Jeanette; Uncle Raymond; Aunt Pauline; Mommy; Daddy; *sitting:* Great-grandpa; Great-grandma

Meet JOSEPH and his family

Joseph lives on a farm with his family, which spans four generations. Great-grandpa bought the land when he was young.

Joseph loves to help on the farm. After school, he feeds the newborn calves. In early spring, the family collects maple sap from the trees in the woods. Then they boil it into sweet syrup in the sugarhouse. During the harvest, Joseph rides with his dad on the big tractor.

It takes the whole family to run this farm.

top: Lindsay; sister Masha; *bottom:* Mommy; Daddy

Meet *Lindsay* and her family

Lindsay and Masha live part of the time with Mommy in her apartment with their cat. The rest of the time they live with Daddy in his apartment with their dog. In both homes they have clothes, toys, and their own bedrooms. With Mommy, they do art and science projects. With Daddy, they play sports and read.

At first the divorce was hard to get used to. But because of their parents' love, they have a happy family life.

sister Ashley; Mom; Tommy

Meet Tommy and his family

Tommy lives in hilly Vermont, where winters are long. He loves to speed downhill on a sled with Mom and Ashley.

Often Tommy visits Pop-Pop, his grandfather, who lives nearby with his goats. Pop-Pop lets Tommy feed the chickens and collect eggs. With the eggs, Mom makes French toast.

Tommy plays often with his sister. Sometimes they fight over toys. But at bedtime, when Mom reads a story, they all cuddle up together.

brother Sherron; Grandma; Christina

Meet Christina and her family

Christina and Sherron live in a city housing project with Grandma. Grandma patrols their building with her neighbors to keep it safe for her grandchildren.

Christina is Grandma's little helper. She gives a hand with chores. But she also loves riding her bike. Christina is proud when Grandma helps her teacher at school outings. Grandma also goes to Sherron's ball games to watch him play and to make sure she knows what he is up to.

Grandma is loving, caring—and strict.

top: foster mother Sela; foster brother Michael; *bottom:* sisters Crystal and Debby; *center:* Isaac; *drawing:* Mom

Meet *Isaac* and his family

Isaac, Crystal, and Debby live with their foster family who love them and care for them. During the week Sela walks them to school. On Sundays, after church, she cooks them delicious Colombian meals.

Michael is like an older brother. He is smart. He helps the children with their schoolwork. Isaac loves best when Michael plays computer games with them.

The children see their real mom once a week. Perhaps in the future they will return to her.

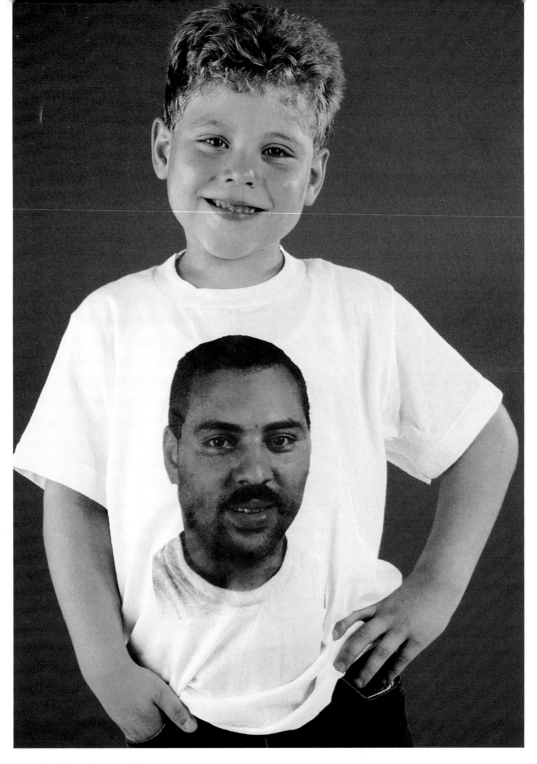

top: Justin; *bottom:* Papa

Meet J u s+i n and his family

Justin lives with his Papa, whom he loves and admires. During work hours, he stays with Mamita, his grandmother, who looks after him. Justin enjoys her tasty cooking. Yellow rice, beans, and chicken are his favorites. With Mamita he speaks Spanish. With Papa he speaks English.

On Papa's days off, they ride bikes and Rollerblade. Justin is strong and athletic, but some days he suffers from asthma. On those days, he and Papa stay home and watch baseball or play board games.

top: Chastidy; *bottom:* Daddy; Nydia; brother Evan

Meet *Chastidy* and her family

When Daddy married Nydia, Chastidy worried about having a stepmother. Would she love Nydia? Would Nydia love her?

Getting to know each other took time and a few tears. But soon Nydia and Chastidy discovered they both love "crazy dancing." They turn up the music loud and twirl and twist through the living room. They also share a secret love for ice cream.

Since they worked together at Nydia's office all summer, Chastidy feels very close to her new mom.

in frame clockwise from top left: brother Imani; mother Susan; father Jahwawa; brother Cyril; baby Nathaniel; sister Marini; *right:* Jahsee

Meet Jahsee and his family

Jahsee's father is of African descent. He comes from the Virgin Islands. Jahsee's mother is Norwegian American. The children are a beautiful combination of both parents. Like their father, the boys often wear traditional African hair locks, called "roots." Jahsee loves to go to the beach with the whole family and play in the sand and the waves. And he can't wait until they all go on a ship to visit Grandma in the Virgin Islands.

back row: Papi; Mami; baby Lillian; *front row:* brothers Julio, Edwin, and Ángel; *right:* Liza

Meet Liza and her family

Liza and her family live in a shelter for homeless families. She misses her old house, her friends, and the toys she lost. But she likes her new day-care center where she sings, plays, and listens to stories.

Mami cooks, washes, cleans, and cares for the children. Papi looks for a job so they can get a nice new home. Every night Liza prays that he'll find one soon.

Liza loves being with her family. They are strong, and they will get over these hard times together.

Mom; Chris; Dad

Meet *Chris* and his family

On most Sundays, Chris and his mom leave their apartment and drive to a big building with iron gates. In a small room, Dad is waiting. They hug each other. Chris settles into his father's lap. For an afternoon they enjoy talking, playing games, and being a family. Too soon, it's time to say good-bye.

Chris knows that his father is in prison because he made a big mistake. He loves and misses his dad and wants him to come home. Chris's karate classes teach him patience.

Daddy; Mommy; Kimberly

Meet *Kimberly* and her family

Kimberly enjoys many activities with her parents. Daddy coaches her soccer games, and Mommy cheers her on. They go on picnics and adventures in the country. Kimberly enjoys dressing up and going to the ballet. And they all adore having high tea with fancy pastries afterwards.

Even though Mommy can't walk, she can go everywhere the family goes with her electric scooter.

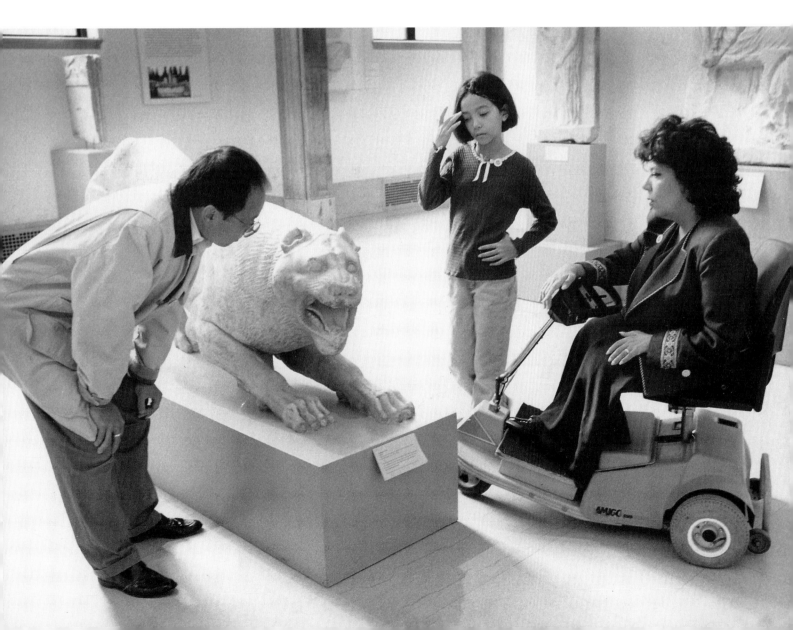

left: Alexandra; *right:* Mama Alice; sister Sarah; Mama Sally

Meet ALEXANDRA and her family

Alexandra loves her family—especially her giggly sister with whom she shares many secrets. Alexandra and Sarah were both born in Brazil. They were adopted when they were babies.

Now they live and go to school in New York City. They are best friends. At home they love to dress up and pretend to be princesses. On weekends they go to the country. There they go exploring in their garden. They also visit with their grandparents and their favorite uncle Jim.

standing: neighbors; *sitting:* Daddy; Emma; Mama

Meet EMMA and her family

Emma picks a carrot for Daddy and a sunflower for Mama from the garden. She is happy in her parents' new house. Friendly neighbors live close by. They all share the land and the big garden. Sometimes they cook and eat together in a house that belongs to all of them.

Emma's neighbors, old and young, play, make music, tell stories, and enjoy one another's company. In this "co-housing" community, everyone lives together like one big, caring family.

MORE ABOUT FAMILIES

Everybody has a family. From the moment we are conceived, we all have a mother and a father. And we are all related to all of our parents' blood relatives through the generations.

But not everyone grows up in the family they began with. Some people live with part of their original family. Some never know their parents. Some go through life having never met a blood relative.

The fourteen children in this book have introduced you to their own unique families. Some of you may have seen a family here that is similar to your own. Some of you may not have. There are many more kinds of families than there are pages in this book.

GLOSSARY

Adopted child - a child who is brought into a family, by legal means, to be raised as its own

Aunt - a mother's or father's sister

Biracial family - a family with members of two different races

Co-housing community - a community where people live separately but share common space, land, and some activities

Cousin - the child of an aunt or an uncle

Divorce - to end a marriage

Extended family - a family made up of parents, brothers and sisters, and other relatives such as grandparents, aunts, uncles, and cousins all living under one roof

Family - a group of people related by blood or marriage; a group consisting of parents or guardians and the children they rear; a group of people living under one roof, forming a household

Father - a male parent (birth father, stepfather, or foster father)

Foster family - a temporary family in a time of crisis

Generation - the span of time between the birth of parents and the birth of their children; children, their parents, their grandparents, and their great-grandparents make up four generations

Grandparent - the parent of one of your parents

Half sister or brother - a sibling who is related through one parent only

Mother - a female parent (birth mother, stepmother, or foster mother)

Nuclear family - a family made up of only a mother, a father, and one or more children

Sibling - a sister or a brother; children who share at least one parent

Single parent - a mother or father who raises a child or children alone without a second parent

Stepfamily - a family that is partly related by blood and partly related by marriage

Uncle - a mother's or father's brother

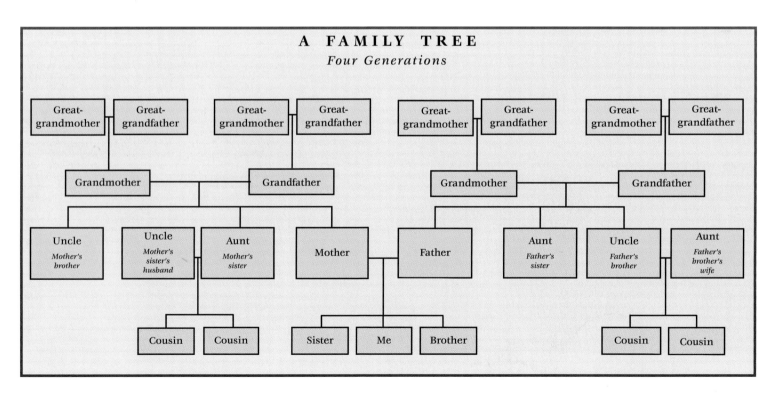

A FAMILY TREE
Four Generations